Four Days at the Pentagon

The Account of One Marine's Service at the Pentagon

9/11/01 – 9/14/01

Jon,

Thank you for making this world a better place!

Semper Fi. & God Bless.

Dan Pantaleo

Dan Pantaleo

Thank you for purchasing this book. Proceeds are used to benefit the Wounded Warrior Regiment.

For more information about supporting the Wounded Warrior Regiment, please go to:

http://www.woundedwarriorregiment.org

ISBN: 1463746032
ISBN-13: 978-1463746032

Table of Contents

1. Foreword, by Sergeant Major Alford McMichael, USMC, ret. (14th Sergeant Major of the Marine Corps) ------------ Page 7

2. Preface --- Page 9

3. Chapter 1- 9/11/01 A Date That Changed America--- Page 11

4. Chapter 2- The Smoke Clears & A Presidential Visit-- Page 33

5. Chapter 3- Stubborn Defiance & The USMC Flag ---- Page 49

6. Chapter 4- The Aftermath -------------------------------- Page 79

7. Acknowledgements -------------------------------------- Page 95

Dedication

This book is dedicated to the 184 honored victims who lost their lives at the Pentagon on 9/11 and to their families. Losing a loved one so tragically but going on to live a life that honors them is courageous, noble, and brave. They are true American heroes.

Secondly, I dedicate this book to the men and women who stand on the fence every day protecting our freedoms. May God bless and watch over them.

Finally, I dedicate this work to my wife and best friend, Jacqueline; my son, Joseph; and my daughter, Amanda.

Foreword

Dan Pantaleo's account of the recovery operations in and around the Pentagon from 9-11-01 until 9-14-01 is a raw, close up view of historical events that essentially changed our way of life in America. While the actions that occurred in New York City have been chronicled in many publications, there are very few first-hand accounts of the recovery efforts that took place at the Pentagon on 9-11 and the days thereafter. *Four Days at the Pentagon* is one of them. From creating the Initial Response and Recovery Mortuary Team to the orderly transition of the recovery work to the Army's Old Guard, this book documents events of historical importance to our nation. The details outlined in this book transport the reader back in time to September 2001 and provide additional insights into events the mainstream media barely touched.

As our nation continues to transform in the wake of the terrorist attacks on 9-11, books like this are important toward understanding how and why America's international engagement policy is formed. Dan Pantaleo, and those who served at the Pentagon, the World Trade Center site, and at Shanksville, Pa. played an important role that typifies the American spirit. It is fitting that this story be told.

Well done, Dan Pantaleo. I will keep this book on the top of my bookshelf.

------Sergeant Major Al McMichael, USMC, ret.
(Sergeant Major of the Marine Corps, 1999-2003)

Preface

In the Hollywood movie Vantage Point, a very high profile event, the assassination of an American president, is shown over and over again from slightly different points of view. Similarly, millions of Americans have slightly different points of view when recalling the highest profile event to occur in the past fifty years, the terrorist attacks on 9/11/2001. In its simplest form, *Four Days at the Pentagon* is one person's point of view of what occurred at the Pentagon on 9/11 and the subsequent three days. However, it is more than just a single point of view; it is a story of the American spirit. It is that intrinsic spirit all of us possess in one form or another: the spirit that demands and takes action in crisis situations, the spirit of pulling together for a common cause, and the spirit of being of service for no other reason than "it seemed like the right thing to do".

The tempo of this book purposefully begins slowly, almost sleepily, just as September 11, 2001 began. However, as the story unfolds the pace moves quickly by design, analogous to our nation's heightened awareness of terrorism.

Chapter 1

9/11/01 A Date That Changed America

Tuesday morning, September 11 to Wednesday morning, September 12

Cresting over the I-395 Bridge near Route 27 in Northern Virginia, the vista of our national fortress, the Pentagon, comes into view. Behind the Pentagon is the Washington Monument and the Capitol building. This image of these three buildings lined up in a row served as a daily reminder that I worked in the most powerful city in the world. The Roman Empire had Rome; the Byzantine Empire had Constantinople; the British Empire had London; and now, in the twentieth and twenty-first centuries, we Americans have Washington DC. I viewed my time working in the Washington area as an honor. My job in the nation's capital was a long way from my humble roots as a blue-collar, Midwestern kid growing up in Roseville, Michigan, and I enjoyed the daily reminder that I was part of this unique workforce.

The path I took to becoming one of the cogs in the

Washington DC machine is not really all that remarkable. After graduating from Olivet College (Olivet, Michigan) in 1985, I sought out a career that would challenge me intellectually, physically, and as a leader. I had been a successful college wrestler, made decent grades, and was deeply interested in history and political science. Consequently, I had to look outside my home state, as there were not very many career opportunities in Michigan for a person with my background and interests. Besides, the challenges of becoming a United States Marine seemed to call out to me and my desire to serve during the Reagan years was quite strong. As the fifth child in a large Italian family of eleven, I learned tenacity, stubbornness, and the ability to thrive in dynamic environments. These traits served me well in the military, and after graduating from the U.S. Marine Corps (USMC) Officer Candidate School in December 1985, I went on to serve the next sixteen years in a variety of assignments that literally took my family and me all over the world. My assignment in the summer of 2001 to the nation's capital was both a pleasure and a privilege.

Tuesday, September 11, 2001, started like most any other day that summer. I drove from my house in Stafford, Virginia, to the commuter parking lot just a few miles down the road and joined one of the ad hoc car pools formed from a system called "slugging"—essentially, I caught a ride to my office in Rosslyn, Virginia, with a car full of strangers. Rosslyn is located in Northern Virginia, about three miles north of the Pentagon, and borders Washington DC. It is considered one of the hubs of the urban layout near the DC area, with numerous skyscrapers that house various federal and high-tech, defense-oriented offices. I walked into the building that morning, took the elevator to the fourth floor, and settled in at my desk for another "exciting" day of pushing paper. As the only active-duty USMC officer of the one hundred people working at the Joint Tactical Radio Systems, Joint Program Office (JTRS, JPO), I had the unenviable job of trying to represent the needs of the USMC warfighting community, while balancing the Joint Service requirements of the JPO. It was a good job in that it was challenging and for a worthy cause, but it was not very exciting. In fact, the assignment to the JPO paled in comparison to my previous duty station, teaching at the U.S. Naval Academy. Mentoring midshipman at the academy was one of the most rewarding experiences of my career.

As enjoyable and challenging as most of my military assignments had been up to that point, my career was still somewhat ordinary. I had never been shot at and was never directly involved in true combat operations, though I had seen my share of Marines die. In March 1989, I participated in a major training exercise in South Korea called "Team Spirit." During this joint/combined exercise, I witnessed one of the most horrific peacetime accidents ever to befall the U.S. Marine Corps when a CH-53 helicopter crashed near Pohang, Korea, with twenty-two Marines on board. All twenty-two lost their lives. I assisted at the crash site, alongside Captain Mike Dana (now a brigadier general) and carried out the tough duty of recovering the remains of my fellow Marines. Little did I know on this fine September morning in 2001 that those same skills and mind-set developed eleven years earlier would be required again.

Later that morning, one of my co-workers, Rosa Baez, the secretary for the JPO's commanding officer, Colonel Steve MacLaird (U.S. Air Force), informed me that some sort of a plane crashed into the World Trade Center building in New York City. Since Colonel MacLaird was on assignment in Sweden and the next-in-line senior officers, Colonel Michael Cox and Lieutenant Colonel (LTC) Robert Heathcock (both U.S. Army) were indispose at meetings; Rosa figured that since I carried the rank of Major, I was next in the chain of command. We listened to the reports as they came over the radio, but none of them gave much detail. We assumed it was a small, private airplane that had probably flown too close to the high buildings and was blown into the structure. Quite frankly, since the initial reports of the plane crash were so sparse on details, we did not think very much of the event even though we were concerned for the possible loss of life. Nonetheless, Rosa turned up the volume of her portable radio, and a short while later, an announcement came across the airwaves that instantly changed our way of thinking. In an excited, frightened tone of voice, the announcer stated that another plane, a large commercial jet, had just crashed into the other tower of the World Trade Center. It was confirmed that both planes had been hijacked. By then, a small crowd of our co-workers had gathered around Rosa's desk. Hushed conversations and shocked looks replaced our previous cavalier attitudes. My thinking instantly changed as well; it was obvious these two events were connected in a coordinated terrorist attack. I began to think about the vulnerability of our building. The Joint Tactical Radio (JTRS) office occupied the entire fourth floor of a rather large, tall building. We turned the volume of the radio up even louder now and listened intently. There was an air of concern and foreboding in the office. As reports trickled in about the situation in New York City, we talked in whispers about what those poor people were experiencing on the upper floors of the Trade Center towers. Then suddenly, from our large bay window, we saw a huge plume of smoke billowing about three miles in the distance. Within a few minutes, that same excited, frightened voice came across the radio to tell us the Pentagon had just been attacked as well. One account indicated it was a bomb, but less than a few minutes later, the reporter confirmed that it was another hijacked airliner. Reports came across the airwaves that the White House and the Capitol building were being evacuated. A day or so later, we would learn the commercial airliner that slammed into the Pentagon, American Airlines Flight 77, was carrying sixty-four people. Among the passengers were young children on their first airplane ride. Over the next few days, the reality of their deaths would have a lasting and haunting impact on me.

Members of the office crowded around the bay window straining to see the effects of the plane crash on the Pentagon. Sudden and deep feelings of despair, shock, concern, and anxiety filled the office. Within the span of just fifty minutes, three hijacked planes had slammed into buildings of national prominence, and our paradigm of an invincible America was suddenly shaken to the core. While my co-workers looked at each other with this "When will the next shoe fall?" expression, I walked down the hall to the large conference room where LTC Heathcock was hosting a conference with local defense contractors. I interrupted the meeting to inform him of the morning's events. After a brief exchange, we agreed that we ought to evacuate our building as well. LTC Heathcock and I came to this decision for two reasons: 1) We figured we could potentially be in danger, considering our building stood atop a major metro hub, and 2) Work was the last place anyone wanted to be after the catastrophic events of the morning.

By this time, the attacks and building evacuations in Washington were being broadcast on every major TV channel and news service. I knew my parents in Michigan and my wife, Jacqueline, in Virginia would probably be wondering about my whereabouts since I frequently attended meetings at the Pentagon. I quickly phoned both of them to let them know I was safe. Interestingly enough, my wife had just returned from her morning bike ride and was completely unaware of the attacks. She turned on the television as we spoke, and the shock, surprise, and dismay in her one-word answers to my questions told me she was quickly being caught up on the events of the day. We agreed to continue the conversation after I evacuated the building. I changed out of my service "C" uniform, put on my civilian clothes, and took one last look at the TV we had on display in the conference room. As I watched the reports of both towers collapsing in New York, a sickening feeling swept over me. The loss of life had to be catastrophic. At this time of the morning, I guessed there must have been nearly five thousand people in those buildings and well over that number in the Pentagon. LTC Heathcock and I made one last sweep through the office to confirm it was empty and made our way to the elevator.

Riding down to the ground floor, I could think of only one thing: I needed to get to the Pentagon and be of whatever assistance I could. I tried to catch a bus or a taxi, but the streets of Rosslyn were in chaos and traffic was completely jammed. It seemed the JPO wasn't the only office to clear out. I began jogging in the direction of the smoking building. While en route, I linked up with a few military doctors and nurses who were moving in the same direction. One of the nurses, Lieutenant Colonel (LTC) Mahee Edmonson, U.S. Army Reserve, asked if I had any identification on me. Considering my ethnic background (Italian and Lebanese) and the civilian clothes I was wearing, I did not view her request as unusual. In fact, her asking to see my ID was a sign of her clear thinking and decision-making, which would prove to be quite valuable over the next four days. After I showed her my U.S. Marine Corps identification, she said, "We can definitely use a Marine at a time like this; would you like to come with us?" We moved out at a fast pace for about ten minutes and then caught a ride with a Navy captain who was driving down a closed road. Actually, he was driving in the wrong direction on a one-way road, but since it was closed off and we were in the midst of chaos, it seemed like the right thing to do. This notion of "it seemed like the right thing to do at the time" became a theme over the next four days. One of the lessons I learned from 9/11 is that in a time of crisis, traditional rules and regulations are more like *guidelines*. We did what we thought needed to be done, and if a rule or regulation stood in the way of progress, we ignored it.

When we reached the Pentagon, we began assembling triage units, and my group coordinated with a cluster of civilian medical professionals who had just arrived from a local hospital. The pungent smell of the burning jet fuel and building material dominated our senses as the intense heat from the fire radiated out to our staging site. We set up our triage materials just under the Route 27 Bridge in the area of the south Pentagon parking lot. The situation was chaotic and various first responders were moving about fast and furious.

Meanwhile my group began to organize personnel into teams, acquire supplies, and attempt to determine who was in charge. I quickly learned that *nobody and everybody* was in charge. If you spoke with authority and had a good idea of how to assist potential victims, people followed you and carried out your orders.

A few days before 9/11, I had read excerpts from Carl von Clausewitz's *On War*, and as I stood amidst the chaos at the Pentagon on the morning of September 11, I could relate to his concept of the "fog of war" (the confusion that is created in combat, which keeps commanders from understanding what is really going on). There were occasional sirens and loudspeaker announcements that another plane was inbound and we should seek shelter away from the Pentagon. Nonetheless, we continued to positioned stretchers, supplies, and sought to get into the burning building to see if we could help. First responders, mostly firefighters and police, set up barriers to keep people back, and within a few hours, LTC Edmonson and I came to the realization that our triage efforts might not be required. With regret, she and I discussed plans for making the transition from providing medical assistance or rescue operations to setting up potential "recovery" operations.

We still clung to the hope that some of the first responders could reach injured victims, so we continued to position personnel and supplies to be of maximum assistance in the event they were needed. However, after such an extended period of time, we had to face the reality of the situation. Nearly five hours after the attack, it was unlikely that people would emerge from the inferno. Consequently, LTC Edmonson and I began coordinating with other volunteers and some of the various organizations represented at the Pentagon to begin the process of recovering the victims.

A recovery operation, similar to the work I performed after the helicopter crash in South Korea back in 1989, would require different types of supplies than what we possessed at that time. It would also require a different mind-set. When one is involved in rescue operations, there is optimism and the hope of finding someone alive. However, when the task becomes recovery versus rescue, the mood becomes tremendously heavy and grim. Some people experience a compartmentalization effect, which permits them to deal with awful situations such as body recovery. I remembered this "compartmentalization" from my time in South Korea and began to make the mental shift I knew would be required. With the assistance of other volunteers, we began to gather the types of supplies to be used in recovery operations.

Again, there did not seem to be any one particular organization in charge. LTC Edmonson and I linked up with members of the Army's Old Guard, the Federal Emergency Management Agency (FEMA), and the Federal Bureau of Investigation (FBI), along with individuals from a variety of organizations. We formed an ad hoc "mortuary affairs / recovery" group, which would later be known as the Initial Response and Recovery Mortuary Team (IRRMT). Over the next four days, I would serve as the Executive Officer of this group while LTC Edmonson took on the Commanding

Officer role. Together, she and I served as military representatives for the recovery efforts carried out at the Pentagon's "ground zero." The group we led was comprised of volunteers, and in the following paragraphs, I describe some of those with whom I worked most closely.

Officer Art Robinson was a sergeant in the Department of Pentagon Security (DPS) and an extremely handy guy to have assisting us. Art was a stocky, confident, muscular police officer, who immediately recognized what LTC Edmonson and I were trying to accomplish. Almost instantly, he and I gelled, and we worked very well together. For the next seventy-two hours, he would serve as my enforcer whenever I needed it. He arranged for police escorts, kept onlookers back, and "encouraged" cooperation from anyone who might otherwise be uncooperative.

David Roth was a director with FEMA, and as the battles over who was in charge of the recovery efforts simmered down, he eventually assumed overall control for the nonmilitary members of the recovery effort. David served as our primary point of contact for coordination with any nonmilitary organizations.

Various members of the FBI joined our team and

provided us with "special" cell phones programmed for priority access on any cell network. Additionally, they established a makeshift forensics office in a private parking garage of the Pentagon, about a mile east of the impact site. Since the Pentagon was technically considered a crime scene, the FBI took jurisdiction over any evidence in the area.

The workers who crawled in and around the Pentagon over the next four days to bring out the victims included members of the Army's Old Guard—Command Sergeant Major (CSM) Butts, Captain Nuremberg, and Staff Sergeant Frazier; U.S. Marines—Captains Wiess, Hansbrough, and Sutton; Gunnery Sergeant Malnichck; Staff Sergeant Mix; Sergeants Chambers and Farrington; Corporals Weintraub, Hashim, and Trimpert; and two people whom I would come to know and work very closely with over the next four days, Eric Jones and Staff Sergeant Chris Braman (U.S. Army).

Eric Jones was a graduate student at George Washington University and a volunteer firefighter during September 2001. He had a calmness about him and an unshakable resolve to accomplish any mission assigned to him. He spoke with a maturity beyond his years (Eric was only twenty-five at the time) and encouraged a sense of cooperation from others. Eric arrived at the Pentagon within a few minutes of the attack and assisted with the evacuation of burn victims. He would serve with distinction at the Pentagon over the next four days and then go on to New York City to assist at the WTC "ground zero" for weeks afterward. Eric was one of just a handful of people to receive the nation's highest civilian award—the Medal of Valor—for his actions at the Pentagon.

Eric Jones

Staff Sergeant Chris Braman, a former special operations soldier, was serving in the U.S. Army's chief of staff office at the Pentagon on September 11, 2001. He was tossed about when the plane crashed into the building but managed to get out unscathed. Then, like many others, he immediately went back into the smoldering structure to search for victims. One of the people he saved was Mrs. Sheila Moody. Mrs. Moody was so badly burned that she could not speak to call out for help. The only thing she was able to do was clap her hands and pray that someone would find her. Chris Braman answered her prayers by continuing to search through the smoke and fire until he located her. Chris relayed to me that she whispered to him, as the fire began to rage, "I'm gonna die."

Chris answered her, "No you aren't - not today" He and Ted Anderson, a retired U.S. Army lieutenant colonel, then carried her to safety where she was taken by ambulance to the hospital. Mrs. Moody suffered badly from her burns but survived to return to a normal life thanks to the heroic efforts of Staff Sergeant Braman and Ted Anderson.

Chris Braman recalled the day's horror:

"It had every bit of the smells of combat. It had the screams; it had the fire, the burns, and the victims' faces. I'll always remember the victims' faces," Braman recalled. "Not only those I saw on the eleventh, but the next three days. I actually saw what death looks like straight in the eyes. I touched it, smelled it, and tasted it. Seconds became minutes, and minutes became hours. The next thing I knew, it was 1:47 in the afternoon. I was very fortunate to get out before that area collapsed. I can't explain why things happen." (www.usma.edu/dcomm/PV/Pentagon.htm).

Staff Sergeant Chris Braman

Chris, Eric, and I began the process of organizing the volunteers into groups of four, staging supplies (stretchers, body bags, fire-retardant suits, and biohazardous material equipment), and carving out an area near the Pentagon's helicopter pad as a base of operations for the recovery team. We commandeered two green general-purpose (GP) military tents and erected them about two hundred yards from the impact site. The next item we commandeered was a large white truck, which had been used to carry frozen goods. The driver was delivering cases of cooled water bottles, soft drinks, and fresh fruit for the hundreds of construction workers, firefighters, police, medical workers, and military volunteers now positioned at the Pentagon's ground zero. The large vehicle was equipped with special air-conditioning units to keep the payload it carried cool or frozen. I asked the driver if he (and the truck) was available to remain on-site a few hours longer, and he informed me that if we needed his truck, it was ours for as long as we required it. The high walk-in covered bed of the vehicle made for a perfect mobile command post, if required. The other reason I wanted this truck was that I figured (rightly so) that we might need it to transport the victims from the Pentagon to a forensics facility or morgue.

By this time, the sun was starting to set and the initial shock of the hijackings was beginning to fade into the focused actions we were undertaking. We worked with purpose as we set up the makeshift command post, comprised of the FEMA reps, the FBI, senior officials from the Pentagon, fire department personnel, building construction crew leaders, and the recovery / morgue team (us). Leaders of the various organizations represented in the Pentagon compound held a meeting at the FBI's large mobile trailer command post. The construction and fire department leadership was adamant that nobody should make attempts to get into the building while it was still unstable and had pockets of fire. We all agreed not to attempt to go into the building until it was deemed safe to enter.

The staging and preparation activates continued for many more hours. We did take time to listen to the President's address to the nation that evening at about 8:30 p.m. Some of the recovery crew leaders piled into the cab of the large white truck, and we tuned the radio in to hear President Bush's speech. The President stated, "Our way of life, our very freedom, came under attack in a series of deliberate and deadly terrorist acts..." He went on to say that our law enforcement and intelligence communities were working to find those responsible and to bring them to justice. These were just the type of words we were hoping to hear. After every major point of his speech, the people gathered around the cab of the truck would let out spontaneous cheers of "Yes!" and "Let's get 'em!"

After the address, we renewed our efforts with a greater sense of urgency. I phoned my wife to tell her about the recovery effort, and that I would not be home until very late. The activity eventually died down around midnight, and I caught a ride back to the commuter parking lot in Stafford. Driving to my house from the parking lot, I felt an overwhelming urge to talk with God. The tragedy of the day's events was sinking-in, and I felt the only way I could be of service at that moment was to pray for the victims, their families, and for our nation. After parking my vehicle in the driveway, I took a few moments to reflect and, like most Americans, felt a crushing sense of sadness. After a short while, I gathered myself in order to present a strong, stable image when I walked into the house. It was about 1:00 a.m. and Jacqueline was awake and still somewhat shaken by what she had seen on TV. We hugged for what seemed like a very long time, talked, and shared what we were feeling. After watching the latest news updates, I finally decompressed and caught a few hours of sleep.

Later that morning, I left my house about 4:30 a.m. and arrived at the Pentagon at 5:15 a.m.; a commute that normally takes nearly 90 minutes was reduced to half that time. I-95 had never been so void of traffic. I could count on one hand the vehicles on the road that morning. Cresting over the I-395 Bridge near Route 27 that morning, I no longer felt the surge of be being part of the Washington DC machine. I felt sorrow, anger, and a need to take action.

Chapter 2

The Smoke Clears & A Presidential Visit

Wednesday morning, September 12 to Wednesday evening, September 12

I linked up again with LTC Edmonson, Eric Jones, and SSGT Chris Braman, and as the sun rose, we made final coordination with the command center to begin the recovery process. The procedure went as follows: We would get a phone call (using the FBI-issued cell phones) from members of the forensics team inside the Pentagon. They would collect any evidence from the various scenes / areas within the building, and then we would send in crews of four-man stretcher teams. The four-man crews went into the damaged building with the body bags and stretchers and placed the victims inside the bag once they were directed to do so by the agents. The FBI used a numbering system to tag and ID the body and bag, which indicated the location within the building where the victims had been found. The crew then brought the victim out to the freezer truck. We loaded the body into the covered bed of the truck where a chaplain, a military doctor, and I would receive them. We handled these honored victims with as much care and dignity as possible. As instructed by CSM Butts, "Bring them out with dignity, feet first, and remember to hold your heads up high and proud." We carefully placed them on the truck and then unzipped the bag. The doctor would confirm they were deceased; I would check the ID tags to ensure they matched, and the chaplain would say a prayer. Then we would zip the bag, prepare for the next body, and repeat the process. When the truck was filled (usually about twelve body bags), we would send word back into the building to momentarily stop the process. We would then transport the victims to the FBI forensics facility, led by a police escort, turn them over to the care of the bureau's forensics team, and return to the damaged portion of the Pentagon to start the process again. The FBI forensics office, located about a half mile from the Pentagon compound, was a makeshift facility carved out from the Pentagon's private parking garage. At this facility, the forensics crew would take possession of the bodies and process them for transportation via helicopter to Dover Air Force Base. Dover has a permanent morgue facility and is the primary location on the east coast that processes military members killed in combat.

The capacity of the truck became an area of contention with the FBI. Certain members of the bureau wanted us to fill the bed of the truck to a greater capacity. In effect, one of the agents asked us to stack the body bags on top of each other. I denied this request and used whatever authority I had, real or perceived, to encourage treating the victims as honorably as possible as opposed to "evidence." We were *not* going to stack bodies on top of each other. After LTC Edmonson and I had a discussion with a few of their team leaders, they rescinded their request and agreed to move out at our pace.

We were fully aware of the time line we were working against. LTC Edmonson and I were both well versed in the four stages of human decomposition (autolysis, putrefaction, carnivores, and diagenesis). The sooner we were able to recover the bodies and get them to the forensics facility, the quicker they could be transported to Dover and stabilized. If we were able to get the intact victims to a permanent morgue facility within five days or so, their loved ones could potentially have an open-casket funeral if they so chose. It would not be very likely that we would come across any intact victims after five days.

One of the first victims we recovered was Matthew

Flocco, a petty officer second class (U.S. Navy). I was surprised at how young and seemingly peaceful he appeared. Looking at his calm, youthful face, I thought about Matt's parents, and then I thought about my own son, Joseph. He was similar to Joseph in that he was a handsome, fit young man with a great deal of potential. Each time we opened the body bags, I was expecting the worst, but in Matthew's case, he seemed to be a boy, just sleeping. I wanted to yell at him to wake up. I felt an aching pain in the pit of my stomach – he was someone's son, friend, or brother. I momentarily crossed a line those working in body recovery should never cross; I personalized and identified with one of the victims. Part of the mental shift from rescue operations to recovery operations that I mentioned earlier is the need to create an emotional boundary between those handling the victims and victims, themselves. Marines are sometimes considered cruel, dark, or uncaring when it comes to the manner in which we refer to our enemies; we "de-humanize" them. Doing so, allows us to make the mental shift from civility to savagery, which is absolutely required to be successful in combat. Similarly, when handling human remains, I found it best to create margins between professional duties and my personal life.

After taking a deep breath and gritting my teeth, I

steadied myself and carried out the tasks I had volunteered to do. Matt's father, a construction engineer who lived in Newark, Delaware, would later request to be transferred to the Pentagon construction crew responsible for rebuilding the damaged portion of the building. He worked tirelessly for months side by side with the other construction workers to have the building 100 percent ready before the first anniversary of the attack. Mr. Flocco is one of the many brave individuals who participated in the post-9/11 activities. Having the Pentagon restored within a year after the attack is a testament to America's strength and resilience.

The process of recovering the victims went on without interruption for nearly fifteen hours that day. Most of the workers involved in this duty barely took time to eat, use port-o-johns, or catch our breath. It was this constant rush to assist and stay busy that allowed us to engage in this arduous task without fully comprehending what was really happening around us. However, in the course of forming the recovery teams, I noticed there was one volunteer, who seemed quite out of place to me.

His name, or at least the name he gave us, was "Bill"—no last name. His facial hair and ponytail told me he was not a military man, but given the fire-retardant suit he wore, I suspected he was with one of the fire and rescue squads. Even as I was becoming quite fatigued from the fifteen hours of heart-wrenching work, I was alert enough to see something was not quite right about this situation. I brought my concerns to LTC Edmonson, and she gently approached "Bill." As it turned out, his wife had worked at the Pentagon, and when she did not come home on the evening of September 11, he came looking for her. She worked in offices located within a few yards of the impact site. He tried to keep this information a secret, but in the course of his conversation with us, he broke down and through his tears explained why he felt he needed to be involved. Fortunately, an army chaplain was nearby, and we escorted Bill to him. Eventually, Bill phoned some friends they gave him a ride home.

Nearly as disturbing as stories like Bill's was the sight of the horribly damaged Pentagon itself. True to its name, the Pentagon is a five-sided, five-story building (including the subground floor), comprised of five rings connected by a series of corridors. The outer ring, known as the "E" ring, was considered prime real estate and was generally reserved for top-level brass. The next four rings—"D," "C," "B," and "A"—become smaller in size toward the core of the building, yet they maintain the same pentagonal shape. The innermost ring, the "A" ring, forms a five-sided border for the five-acre, open-air interior courtyard, which is filled with trees, bushes, flower gardens, and park benches. The building, which houses its own shopping mall, serves as the headquarters for the Department of Defense and employs nearly twenty thousand people, almost the equivalent population of Bangor, Maine. There are hallways in the Pentagon large enough to drive a full-sized car through.

The section of the building where the plane impacted along the "E" ring looked as if it had been turned upside down and inside out. As I crawled over the concrete rubble and debris to get to some of the locations with our stretcher teams, I could not help but observe how badly damaged our national fortress was. Wires, cables, and steel rods jutted out from every possible angle of the walls, floors, and ceilings. In fact, it was nearly impossible to tell where the ceilings, walls, and floors had once stood. The trips into and out of the damaged area were made even more treacherous by the tons of water that had been sprayed on the jet-fuel fire the day before. The debris smoldered, and hazardous material was everywhere. Masks and fire-retardant suits were mandatory for anyone getting remotely close to the impact site.

The airplane struck in such a way as to cause a deep gash in the structure that penetrated completely through the "E," "D," and parts of the "C" rings. The plane hit at the ground-floor level of the building, but the ensuing fire caused catastrophic damage to all four floors above the impact site, stretching out along the entire southwest portion of the Pentagon. The roof over the impact site collapsed a short time after the crash and formed a sheared-off portion of the building with the collapsed roof and floors down along one side. This image of our national fortress in such a state stood in stark contrast to the powerful building and the worldwide strength it had previously represented. I found the sight sickening.

As the shock of the attacks sank in and the adrenalin of being involved in the crisis began to fade, the recovery crew was becoming noticeably fatigued, irritable, and depressed. Late that afternoon, word traveled throughout the compound that President George W. Bush and Secretary of Defense Donald Rumsfeld would make a visit to the Pentagon. I met President Bush a few months earlier at the U.S. Naval Academy. He delivered the commencement speech there on May 25, 2001, and he took the time to say hello and greet those of us responsible for setting up the event. Regardless of political affiliation, being in the presence of the United States President is a unique and memorable experience for most people. I remembered how inspiring it was to shake his hand and share a few words with him. I thought if the opportunity presented itself when he was at the Pentagon, I would try to get him or Mr. Rumsfeld to visit the recovery teams and maybe share some encouraging words.

The President, his Secret Service entourage, Donald Rumsfeld, National Security Advisor Condoleezza Rice, and a few others arrived without a great deal of fanfare. As they began to walk throughout the compound, a group of firefighters, construction workers, and military personnel on the roof of the intact area of the Pentagon unfurled one of the largest American flags I had ever seen. It gently unrolled and flowed down nearly three stories from the roof, and the people within the compound began to cheer. As President Bush looked up to see the flag unfolding, the crowd began singing "God Bless America." This spontaneous event was totally unscripted and seemed to lift everyone's spirit. The large American flag stood as a patriotic symbol on the Pentagon for the next thirty days and was ceremoniously removed by members of the army's Old Guard on October 11.

After the song was finished, I made my way to one of the President's advisors, Joe Hagin. I explained to him who I was and the job the recovery team was carrying out, and then asked him if the President could quickly meet with the members of my crew. He walked over to the President and whispered something in his ear. The Commander In Chief looked over at the morgue crew and me and then began to walk toward us. Right then, I realized what a sight we must have been to him. As he later described us in his book *Decision Points* we were "covered in dirt after performing the saddest duty of all" (George W. Bush, Decision Points Crown Publishing Group, 2010, pg 142). I tried to wipe my hands clean before shaking his hand, but he was in front of me before I could slap the dust and dirt off. He grabbed my hand and said, "Major, what do we have going on here?" I introduced myself and reminded him that we had met in May at the Naval Academy commencement ceremony. He recalled being at the academy but confessed he did not remember meeting me. Given my ragged appearance now, as I shook his hand, I figured he might remember me this time. I gave the President a quick briefing on our activities and then escorted him down the line as he shook each crewmember's hand.

President Bush thanked us for the dignity we brought to the job we were doing and for our willingness to carry out the task. He explained how important our activities were to the country and especially to those who had lost loved ones the day before. His short speech to the recovery team had the desired effect. To say the crew received a well-timed morale boost is an understatement. As Eric Jones later wrote: "The words of the President and members of his cabinet did wonders to lift our spirits, and it helped give us the strength and courage to continue with the recovery operation" (ABCNews.com *"Diary of Sept. 11 Pentagon Hero"*).

After meeting with the President, members of the recovery crew came to me and expressed their appreciation for having arranged the visit. I felt humbled by this gesture. These young men and women voluntarily stepped up to perform an arduous duty, working in the most difficult circumstances, and here they were expressing thanks to me. The President said we were "instruments of our national resolve" and I was honored to be among these men and women. Once the VIPs left the compound, we returned to our work with a greater sense of purpose.

As the sun set on September 12, the FBI forensics unit was forced to cease their operations because of the hazardous conditions in the Pentagon. Lighting units were erected, but due to the unstable condition of the building, we were unable to get them into positions that allowed the agents to carry out their duties until the next morning. Since the attack, we had recovered approximately forty-eight victims. I say "approximately" because in some cases, we were unable to determine whether we had recovered a full person. The conversations that took place between the forensic agents and those of us carrying out the recovery efforts bordered on the surreal. One agent asked me to double-check bag ID number E-XX-12. "If there is a torso in that bag, then this," he said, holding up a pink bio-hazmat bag containing a severed arm, "belongs with it." I quickly unzipped E-XX-12 and checked.

"Yes, a torso," I called out as I reached to take the bio-hazmat bag into my hands. At the time, we were operating in an adrenaline-fueled, mission-oriented mode and did what needed to be done. It was only days—and in some cases, years—later that the surreal nature of these conversations sank in.

Throughout much of the evening of the twelfth, we resupplied the recovery team with suits, masks, and other equipment. The Red Cross and Salvation Army were instrumental in providing the construction crews, first responders, and our recovery teams with basic creature comforts. Before 9/11, I never fully understood the role of the Salvation Army and the type of support they can provide in a disaster. Now, after having firsthand experience with them, I refuse to walk by their holiday season "bell ringers" without making a contribution. We continued to improve the recovery team command post by setting up cots to sleep on, radios, chalkboards, and supplies. By midnight, the activity ceased again, and I left for my house in Stafford.

Like the night before, I arrived home at about 1:00 a.m., spoke with my wife for a few minutes, and then tried to catch a few hours of sleep. The day's images continued to replay in my head, and after a couple of hours of restless sleep, I woke up, put on a fresh set of camouflage utilities and headed out the door. As I made my way through my small subdivision, I noticed the American flags displayed on the houses. If the terrorists were seeking to change America, in one sense, they succeeded. As the country music singer Toby Keith put it: "This big dog will fight, if you rattle his cage." There were senior officials planning the American response, and I wanted to be part of it. Like many other U.S. citizens, I had never felt so proud to be an American. The Red Cross and blood banks across the country had lines of people seeking to donate blood; phones at military recruiting stations were ringing off the hooks; and a wave of patriotism swept across the United States. September 11 has been described as our generation's Pearl Harbor; this series of terrorist attacks galvanized our national pride in a way I had never seen before and have not seen since.

Chapter 3- Stubborn Defiance & the USMC Flag

Thursday morning, September 13 to Friday afternoon, September 14

About an hour before sunrise on September 13, LTC Edmonson and I began forming the stretcher-carrying teams once again. I linked up with some FBI forensic agents who were new to the compound, and we reviewed our intended activities for the day. Now that the building was no longer smoldering, we would be able to access parts of the structure that had previously been off-limits. Starting at 6:30 a.m., we began the process of staging the white freezer truck, sending in crews, bringing out the victims, and transporting them to the forensics lab. By noon that morning, we had recovered an additional thirty-nine victims, bringing the total number to approximately eighty-seven. Through coordination with FEMA and military command centers, which were located in large white trailers next to our GP tents, I learned the total count was expected to be 184 honored victims, plus five terrorists. After working practically nonstop for nearly fifty hours, we were not quite at the halfway point of the recovery efforts. However, it was becoming obvious the crews we were sending into the structure were getting close to recovering some of the victims on the plane. Even now, years later, I find it challenging and heart-wrenching to accurately describe the condition of the victims we began to recover by the afternoon of the 13th.

One area within the Pentagon that was particularly hard hit was the Navy Command Center (NCC), where approximately 40 bodies were found. Nearly all of the IRRTM volunteers, including myself, donned the plastic coveralls, rubber boots, goggles, and masks and journeyed into the this area of the Pentagon to lend a hand. Crawling in and around the tight spaces and congested passageways was a dangerous undertaking. The unusually hot weather caused our goggles to fog up and we had to be careful not to bump into jagged glass or iron rods protruding from the structure.

Many of the victims we recovered in the early stages of the operation had succumbed to smoke inhalation. The two signs of death by smoke inhalation are the obvious lack of trauma to the victim's body and the unmistakable soot around the nose and face area. However, by the third day, we were able to recover victims who were much deeper in the building; these were victims of severe or catastrophic trauma and burns. Nearly all of the passengers on Flight 77 fell into this category. As we began to recover their remains, and the remains of those within the Pentagon that died of burns, the magnitude of the horrific attack tore at our souls. Bodies seemed to be frozen in a charred state, where limbs were locked and brittle to the touch. We had to be particularly careful with how we handled and moved these remains.

By noon on the third day of operations, the lack of sleep, the draining nature of the work, and the heat of the day were beginning to take their toll again on the psyches of the recovery crew. There was a small green command post (CP) tent manned by military chaplains, who were on standby to provide counseling services to anyone who required them. I remembered this same type of operation from the 1989 accident in South Korea, and just like then, I was too busy to think about talking with a chaplain. However, LTC Edmonson and I kept a close eye on the younger, less experienced volunteers. Whenever it appeared they were having issues with what they were seeing and doing, we encouraged them to visit the chaplain's tent. In some cases, the volunteers returned after the counseling sessions; in other cases, they did not.

Chaplain's tent at the Pentagon, September 12, 2001

Just after noon on the thirteenth, we had a momentary break in our activities. After removing my coveralls, I sat on the bed of the truck with my legs dangling off the edge and watched as Eric Jones and Chris Braman slumped in exhaustion next to me. We took in the sights of the demolition and construction crews attempting to clear out the debris. Eric cracked open a Gatorade bottle, and we passed it around. Our heads were down, and we were too tired to speak. Then, as if guided by an unseen force, Eric and Chris looked up at the gash in the building and saw an amazing and beautiful sight. In front of us, hidden from most angles, standing proud and tall amongst the total devastation on the fourth floor was an intact United States Marine Corps flag.

Eric tapped me on the shoulder and pointed at the flag. We stared at it for what seemed like five minutes. "Well, I'll be damned," I remember saying. "How in the hell...?" I mumbled, and Chris finished my statement, "...did that thing survive?!" Just like the large American flag rolled down from the roof the day before, this USMC flag was an inspiring, heartwarming symbol and gave us something to rally around.

Despite being less than two feet from the sheared line where the walls had collapsed, the flag had withstood a plane crash, flying debris, a voracious conflagration fueled by thousands of pounds of jet fuel, a collapsing wall, secondary fires, secondary collapses, smoke, water, and initial demolition work. Though it was just a piece of cloth, what it stood for that morning is something none of us will ever forget. For us, feeling a little beaten and drained, that flag represented good smirking in the face of evil; hope gently waving off despair; life vehemently opposing death; and triumph standing alone, stubbornly defiant over defeat. Seeing that flag, positioned as it was, lifted our spirits, renewed our energy, and served as an example of our country's resilience and fighting spirit. In an attempt to capture what we were experiencing at that moment, we moved closer to take photographs and get a better view.

USMC flag on fourth floor of damaged Pentagon

I looked over at Chris and Eric and asked with a wry smile, "Are you guys thinking what I'm thinking?" While we had known each other for only a couple of days, we had worked so closely together that we were able to anticipate each other's thoughts and moves. The three of us made our way to the construction crew tent and inquired about retrieving the flag. A crane operator who said his name was "Turkey" told us that within a day or so, this particular portion of the building was going to be demolished and the flag was likely to wind up in the trash heap. My heart sank. After all of the horrific destruction we had seen in the past few days, the three of us agreed it would be a shame to see this symbol of strength and resilience become another casualty.

Just after the conversation with Turkey, my cell phone rang; it was the unit chief with FBI forensics. He explained that the recovery operations would not resume for another sixty to ninety minutes in order to allow crews time to shore up the damaged structure in the next area of the Pentagon to be cleared. This was our chance. The three of us made our way to the command center, and I inquired about retrieving the flag. While everyone agreed it would be great for the morale of the people working in the compound, they were concerned about the safety of those climbing up the structure and asked us to wait a day or two. The trouble with waiting was that the demolition work had already begun, and the flag was so close to the edge that we feared it would fall into the smoldering rubble pile below. We needed to recover the flag safely and in a way that did not interfere with ongoing work.

I linked up again with two of the Marines working the

recovery efforts, Captain Hansbrough and Sergeant Chambers, and explained the mission of salvaging the flag. Chambers suggested forming a human pyramid to "get that flag" if need be. While I appreciated his gung-ho attitude, I was not going to sanction the human pyramid idea. I returned to the original crane operator, Turkey, and asked him about attaching one of the capsulated red baskets and hosting someone up to retrieve the flag. It did not take much to convince him to give the idea a try. He climbed aboard the operators' seat of the crane and began to maneuver it over the red basket. He hooked it up and then returned to where we were standing. "Okay, fellas, who wants to take the ride up?" he called out.

I viewed the privilege of retrieving the flag as a special assignment, and wanted to give that honor to one of the hard-charging enlisted Marines. I asked Sergeant Chambers and Corporal Hashim if either of them would like to carry out the mission. Captain Hansbrough, Eric Jones, and Chris Braman suggested to the Marines that they should consider having me get the flag. As Eric later wrote:

> "Major Dan Pantaleo had been working tirelessly with mortuary affairs doing body recovery and in the refrigeration truck with the doctors. The refrigeration truck was the worst experience because those working in the truck had to view every body and

every body part that came out of the building. The Major was great at organizing recovery operations, communicating with fire department and law enforcement agencies, and looking after the rescue workers. He helped arrange for President Bush to come over and speak with a few of us. This meant a lot to us…" (ABCNews.com *"Diary of Sept. 11 Pentagon Hero"*)

The enlisted Marines overwhelmingly agreed, and they escorted me to the red basket that was hooked to the crane. Standing five feet eight inches, with a limited wingspan, I was not entirely sure I was the right person for this particular job and even mentioned that perhaps the nearly six-foot-tall Hansbrough would be a better choice. However, by then, Eric and Chris had rounded up tools like a garden hoe and a curved crowbar to reach out and pull the flag in and handed them to me. As I was hoisted up, I had a bird's-eye view of the compound and saw that a new group of dignitaries, dressed in suits, was being escorted around the compound. It appeared to be Speaker of the House Dennis Hastert and Senator Joe Lieberman. Since most of the action around the Pentagon had come to a halt, the "floating red basket" became the center of attention. I remember thinking to myself, *Better not screw this up, buddy.* Turkey skillfully maneuvered the basket into position, and I reached out with the hoe. I was able to touch the flag and the pole holder, but it was still too far away for me to pull it in. I heard a noticeable groan from the group watching below. I yelled down to Turkey, "Closer! Take me in another foot!" I reached out again; this time, I had a good handle on the flag. It tipped toward the edge of the building and appeared for a second as if it was going to cascade down into the debris. I leaned over the edge of the basket, bracing my foot against the far wall, and snatched the flag with my hand. I leaned back into the basket, and as the flag was pulled in, the crowd below erupted in cheers.

Pulling in the Marine Corps Colors

As Turkey lowered the basket, people were clapping and cheering. I was filled with a sense of relief and accomplishment, as I watched the VIPs making their way through the crowd toward the base of the crane. After the basket landed, Speaker of the House Hastert and Senator Lieberman came forward to talk with me. I took off my gloves and hard-hat and shook hands with the VIPs. For the second time in as many days, I was standing before senior government officials and was expected to provide an impromptu brief. However, this time, the moment was filled with the excitement and the joy of having salvaged a symbolic item, the USMC flag. All of us smiled broadly, as we shook hands. I introduced myself to Representative Hastert by saying, "Hello, Coach, I'm Major Dan Pantaleo." I knew Dennis Hastert had spent decades as a high school wrestling coach and actually preferred to be called "Coach" by former wrestlers. With the hard-hat off and my cauliflower ears exposed, I was hoping he would recognize me as a former grappler. He did, and we exchanged a few warm words about wrestling and the USMC flag. He finally asked me what I planned to do with the flag, and I was a little worried that he expected me to present it to him. "Well, sir," I went on loud enough so that everyone nearby could hear me, "I'm going to walk this flag up to the Navy Annex and deliver it to the Commandant of the Marine Corps."

The Marines nearby let out a whopping, "Ooooorahhhh!" cheer, and the Speaker smiled and laughed, saying, "Well then, carry on, Marine, carry on."

Chris, Eric, Jared Hansbrough, and I walked out of

the compound toward the Navy Annex. I handed my FBI-issued cell phone to Captain Hansbrough and asked him to call the Commandant's office. I doubted the Commandant of the Marine Corps (CMC) would be available within the ten minutes it would take us to walk to the Annex, but I was hoping at least to put the flag into the hands of a general-level officer. About halfway to our destination, near Route 27, we passed the area where the press corps had been staged for the past two days. It seemed as if every media outlet was represented: *Washington Post* reporters (and photographers), CNN film crews, and even *Stars and Stripes* reporters.

Walking out of the Pentagon compound

As we neared the media crews, my initial instinct was to find a different route to the Navy Annex so we could bypass the press. I know they have a job to do, but as a career military man, I am a little skeptical of the agendas put forward by most media sources. I have always believed the reporters' top concerns are ratings or selling newspapers, and sometimes the average Joe can get crushed in the process.

Nonetheless, the media crews were relentless, and they shouted questions at us and pointed cameras in our direction. Eric, Chris, and I had a quick conversation as we walked in the general vicinity of the press corps. We considered trying to find a more inconspicuous route to the Annex but eventually decided that since salvaging the flag was a good news story, we should make a short diversion over to the reporters. As we neared the area sectioned off by yellow police tape designed to keep the media away from the Pentagon compound, we were suddenly mobbed with cameras, microphones, and questions. Continuously running through my head was, *How might these reporters turn this situation into an ugly story?* I felt guarded in what to say to the media. For example, I did not want to let them know that our real purpose at the Pentagon was the body recovery operations. In some small way, I felt calling the media's attention to the recovery work we were doing betrayed an unspoken code amongst the morgue team. We did not volunteer for that job to gain media attention.

At the media area (damaged Pentagon in the background)

Eric and Chris broke off and told some of the reporters the story associated with the flag. That encouraged a new round of questions. A CNN film crew came over, and as the reporter placed a microphone in front of me, I took the opportunity to give a pep talk. "This flag, found on the fourth floor of the damaged Pentagon, stands in stubborn defiance to what took place here a few days ago. Take a good look at this flag. There isn't a mark, a scratch, nothing on it. It's in pristine condition. Stubborn defiance, I tell ya!" Obviously, emotions were starting to get the better of me. Fortunately, I kept moving toward the Navy Annex as I spoke and the camera crews were unable to keep up, so I was out of range before I could make any other emotionally charged statements. I thought back to the time I had heard General Carl Mundy (CMC from 1991 to 1994) speak to the career officer-level class I attended at Communications Officer School. He said we should never put ourselves into a position that might embarrass the Marine Corps. As I walked up the hill outside the Navy Annex, I thought about what we said on camera and how it might be edited. The last thing I wanted to do was embarrass the USMC.

As we approached the gates of the Navy Annex, a *Stars and Stripes* reporter / photographer hiked alongside us. He continued to pepper us with questions and take photos. I was a little less guarded with the *Stars and Stripes* since they are a military-orientated publication, so I continued the pep talk. He asked me if I had a message for the men and women in uniform who would see this footage. I said, "Tell 'em to get ready for action. America is strong, and we are *not* gonna let those bastards get away with this crap!" Those may not have been the most eloquent words ever to leave my lips, but at least it was out of my system and it felt good to say.

Captain Hansbrough, who had been burning up the phone line the entire walk up to the Navy Annex, informed me there would be a four-star general present to accept the flag. The assistant Commandant, General Michael Williams, was making plans to greet us just outside the main entrance. For a guy who preferred a low profile, I was certainly getting more than my share of face time with the Washington-area brass. General Williams came out of the building accompanied by a few other senior officers and some senior executive service (SES) personnel. I held the flag at a sixty-degree angle and came to the position of attention. General Williams slapped me on the shoulder and shook my hand. He said, "I'll take her from here, Major." Eric, Chris, and Captain Hansbrough were standing just behind me and off to the side. The photo of this event, taken by the *Stars and Stripes* reporter, wound up on the cover of the Naval Academy's *Shipmate* magazine.

Photo of *Shipmate* cover (November 2001)

The General took possession of the flag and said a few words to the members of the media who had gathered. Then, he turned around and presented the flag to SES-4 Peter Murphy, saying, "Sir, I believe this belongs to you." Mr. Murphy served as the senior legal advisor to the

Commandant, and the flag came from his office. In fact, he was in the Pentagon and was slightly injured when the attack occurred.

Peter Murphy's escape from the Pentagon is quite a story in itself. He and Major Joseph D. Baker were having a discussion in Mr. Murphy's office on the fourth floor of the Pentagon's outermost ring, the E-Ring, overlooking the helipad. With CNN on a TV monitor across the room, they stopped their discussion when the news came on concerning the World Trade Center attacks. After watching awhile, Mr. Murphy asked Robert Hogue, his deputy counsel, to check with their administrative clerk, Corporal Timothy Garofola, on the current security status of the Pentagon. Garofola had just received an e-mail from the security manager to all Department of Defense employees that the threat condition remained "normal." He passed this information to Hogue, who stepped back into the doorway of Mr. Murphy's office to relay the message. At that instant, a tremendous explosion with what Mr. Murphy said was a noise louder than any noise he had ever heard shook the room.

The wall moved in, and Mr. Murphy was thrown across the room. The ceiling fell down, and the floor started to buckle. He and several colleagues scrambled into the hall, where they faced a terrifying choice: To their right, there was fire. To their left, there was thick smoke. A voice in the smoke said, "Follow me," and they did. As they were escaping, they heard what they thought was a second plane hitting the building; it was actually the sound of part of the building, including a portion of Mr. Murphy's office, collapsing.

Mr. Peter Murphy, Counsel to the CMC

After transferring the custody of the flag to General Williams, there was no longer a need for Chris, Eric, and me to be present at the Navy Annex, and we were eager to get back to the Pentagon to continue the work we had started. We left quietly and unceremoniously and walked back to the compound. On the way back, I made a couple of quick phone calls to my wife and a few friends to let them know I was involved in an incident that might result in little news coverage. I would find out later that evening that "a little news coverage" was a slight understatement.

CNN showed the news clip of us walking up the road with the flag and of my "stubborn defiance" comment several times that evening. Other major news outlets ran with the story as well. The next morning, on the front page of the *Washington Post*, there was the picture of Eric, Chris, Captain Hansbrough, and me walking along with the flag. I am sure the *Post* photographer took a number of photos of us, but the one they chose to use on the front page of their September 14 edition showed me taking off my mask while walking and holding the flag. At first glance, the photo appears to catch me dabbing my eyes with a tissue. In reality, I was taking off the small mask I wore around my neck. True to form, the *Post* slightly exploited our image in an attempt to portray a tearful emotion from one of the Pentagon workers—in this case, me. It did not matter. I was proud to be part of the flag recovery, and the ensuing article that accompanied the photo talked about the morale boost achieved by salvaging the flag. What none of us counted on was the effect recovering the flag would have on other people, especially the hundreds of rescue personnel, firefighters, law enforcement officers, military personnel, construction workers, politicians, and civilians at the site. Prior to the flag incident, most of the workers within the Pentagon compound seemed to experience various levels of disappointment, grief, and despair. I know I did. However, after we retrieved the flag there was a sense of pride, determination, and, most importantly, hope among the workers.

Weather
Today: Sunny late.
High 68, Low 50.
Saturday: Mostly sunny.
High 70, Low 50.
Details, Page B8

The Washington Post

FINAL

Inside: Weekend
Today's Contents on Page A2

FRIDAY, SEPTEMBER 14, 2001

25¢

CIA's Covert War on Bin Laden

Agency Has Had Green Light Since 1998, but Terrorist Proves Elusive

By Bob Woodward and Vernon Loeb
Washington Post Staff Writers

The CIA has been authorized since 1998 to use covert means to disrupt and prevent terrorist operations planned abroad by Saudi extremist Osama bin Laden under a directive signed by President Bill Clinton and reaffirmed by President Bush this year, according to government sources.

U.S. intelligence has observed the elusive multimillionaire, thought to

be hiding in the mountains of Afghanistan, several times this year, one source said, adding that this holds out the prospect that military strikes could be directed against him.

But reliable intelligence on the whereabouts of bin Laden, who was fingered yesterday by Secretary of State Colin L. Powell as a prime suspect in Tuesday's suicide attacks against the World Trade Center and the Pentagon, has been rare, despite what one source called a "rich and active" surveillance program.

"We have a hell of a targeting problem," the source said, noting that Pentagon analysts are attempting to match current intelligence with military capabilities contained in contingency plans for striking terrorist groups. Those analysts, the source said, are trying to determine whether to attempt to strike bin Laden directly, or to target military action against his aides, training camps, or the broader global network known as al Qaeda, which has connections to other Middle East terrorist groups.

One well-placed source said last night that intelligence gathered since Tuesday's attacks indicates that bin Laden's camps in Afghanistan may be like training centers throughout the Middle East. Are now virtually empty. In addition, Iraqi President Saddam Hussein has moved military equipment this week, as he frequently does when he anticipates U.S. military action, the source said.

The new information on bin Laden comes as the Pentagon reviews plans for what Deputy Defense Sec-

retary Paul D. Wolfowitz described yesterday as a "broad and sustained" campaign against those responsible for Tuesday's attacks and any government found to have provided them sanctuary.

"I think one has to say it's not just simply a matter of capturing people and holding them accountable, but removing the sanctuaries, removing the support systems, ending states who sponsor terrorism," Wolfowitz said. "And that's why it has to be a

See MILITARY, A4, Col. 1

Reliable intelligence on Osama bin Laden has been rare, although he has been observed this year.

Armed Groups Caught Boarding N.Y. Flights; U.S. Readies for War

Bush Pledges Victory; Reagan National Closed Indefinitely

By David Von Drehle
Washington Post Staff Writer

President Bush promised triumph in "the first war of the 21st century" yesterday, as the threat of further terrorist attacks disrupted another day in Washington and clouded efforts to restore the country to a more normal life.

Such was the grim harvest of Tuesday's assaults with hijacked jets on the World Trade Center and the Pentagon. Officials here and in New York indicate the death toll from the attacks is likely to approach—or even exceed—5,000.

"Now that war has been declared on us, we will lead the world to victory," said Bush, whose very visible emotions yesterday ranged from warm tears to cool fury.

Commercial airplanes began flying again yesterday morning on a still-limited basis, but Reagan National Airport remained closed indefinitely. And even this half-step toward normalcy was followed by a wave of further cancellations out of respect for the dead or concern over new threats of violence anew violence.

The leading stock exchanges will remain closed today, with plans to reopen on Monday, amid blocks from the stupefying, still-smoldering heaps of wreckage in Manhattan. Three television networks—ABC, CBS and NBC—postponed the opening of their new television seasons. Most professional sports—Major League Baseball, the National Football League, the PGA Tour, professional soccer—canceled their weekend schedules.

"We tried to be sensible, sensitive and right," said NFL Commissioner Paul Tagliabue.

The Pentagon took a tangible step toward war yesterday, requesting authorization from the White House to call up more than 40,000 reservists. It appeared as expected, the first wave of reservists could be ordered to active duty next week, a senior military official said.

The call-up will be paid for with some of the $40 billion in emergency spending that Congress agreed to yesterday—half

See ATTACK, A20, Col. 1

Dan Pantaleo, a Marine, carries a Marine Corps flag recovered from the Pentagon. With him are civilian firefighter Eric Jones, left, Army Staff Sgt. Chris Braman and Capt. Jared Hansbrough. They delivered the flag to Gen. Michael Williams, Marine Corps assistant commandant.

190 Believed Dead in Pentagon Attack

By Carol Morello and Steve Vogel
Washington Post Staff Writers

The loss became official yesterday: Tuesday's attack on the Pentagon made it the region's bloodiest day since the Civil War.

As the government announced that 190 people were believed to have died when a jet crashed into the Pentagon, two-person teams of soldiers fanned across the region to officially notify families that relatives who had been listed on

duty could not be located.

Rescue workers who had been digging feverishly for two days described eerie scenes of offices seemingly untouched by the plane crash or the resulting fire, while around them was total destruction.

But even in the ruins, there were small moments that seemed to lift morale. A Marine Corps flag that somehow survived the inferno was carefully carried away yesterday afternoon before a row of soldiers saluting in defiant pride.

"When you look at the destruction in

there, it's like walking in hell," said Command Sgt. Maj. Aubrey Butts, of the Army's "Old Guard" at Fort Myer, as he stood yards from the pancaked layers of concrete. "You just look and know? It was horrible for the people who were in there."

A coordinator of the Army's search and rescue teams said workers had placed remains of about 60 corpses in body bags by yesterday morning. In the afternoon, Army Huey helicopters began ferrying them to Dover Air Force Base in

See PENTAGON, A23, Col. 1

■ Pentagon rescuers struggle through a grisly task. | Page B1

FBI Links 16 In Tuesday's Terror Strikes To Bin Laden

By Dan Eggen and Peter Slevin
Washington Post Staff Writers

Authorities detained two armed groups at New York airports yesterday, fearing they intended to hijack a pair of jetliners and mount another suicidal terrorist strike on a U.S. target, government officials said.

Both groups carried knives, false identification and open tickets to U.S. destinations dated Tuesday—the day of the attacks on the World Trade Center and the Pentagon, sources said. They also had certificates from a Florida flight training school attended by some members of the previous hijacking teams, who were similarly armed when they commandeered four aircraft.

Jim Hunter, a passenger on an American Airlines flight scheduled to leave John F. Kennedy International Airport in Los Angeles yesterday, said officers with guns drawn stormed the flight from the front and rear at about 8 p.m. They handcuffed and removed three people after ordering all passengers to the floor. The flight was canceled.

The FBI said yesterday it had identified at least 18 hijackers who had conducted Tuesday's suicidal assaults. Sixteen of them have been directly or indirectly linked to the terrorist network run by Saudi fugitive Osama bin Laden, according to a government source.

Authorities expanded their hunt for accomplices of the hijackers, a quest that now stretches to Germany, where police said they were tracking alleged members of a cell created by the terrorists responsible for Tuesday's assaults.

A coordinated and long-running conspiracy, authorities believe, led to the attacks that killed thousands. The teams that hijacked the four jetliners Tuesday include men with pi-

See PROBE, A19, Col. 3

■ Patterns begin to emerge among suspects. | Page A18

Analysis

Crisis Brings Shift In Presidential Style

By Dana Milbank
Washington Post Staff Writer

For his first eight months in office, President Bush has made since Tuesday's attacks from emphasizing an America "open for business" to portraying himself as a commander in chief for what will likely be a long struggle. Speaking bitterly of those who "hate our values" and "hate what America stands for," he swept aside his beloved domestic policy priorities.

Standing behind him in the Oval Office, a strikingly combative and emotional Bush vowed to lead the nation and an allied coalition to victory over international terrorists and their sponsors. "Now is an opportunity for this generation of a how, by coming together and whipping terrorism, hunting it down, finding it and holding them accountable," Bush said.

The moment was part of a sharp pivot Bush has made since Tuesday's attacks from emphasizing an America "open for business" to portraying himself as a commander in chief for what will likely be a long struggle.

"The nation must understand, this is now the focus of my administration," he said. "Now that war has been declared on us, we will lead the world to victory." It served as an

See BUSH, A13, Col. 1

President and Laura Bush visited attack victims at Washington Hospital Center.

New York's Firefighters Grieve for Lost Brothers

By Anne Hull
Washington Post Staff Writer

NEW YORK, Sept. 13—The firefighters from Engine 202 in Brooklyn called themselves the brothers from Red Hook. At the firehouse, they tried out new recipes on one another. They named their softball team the Red Hook Raiders and started a cigar club that allowed them to puff on Macanudos at their adopted hangout, Smokey's.

On Tuesday, seven of them disappeared in the World Trade Center inferno.

Where, Tony Catapano wondered, did his brothers go?

For 39 years, Catapano has survived his line of work. He is 61, with gray hair and a pension within reach. He is old and they were

young. He showed them how to make meatballs and how to find fire hidden in a wall.

Today he walked near the smoldering landscape of rubble and kept thinking he would see them, shimmying flashlights miraculously from a crevice.

He looked for Tommy Kennedy, Terry McShane, Patrick Byrd, Joe Maffeo, Brian Cannizzaro, Salvatore Calabro and Joe Gullickson.

Even as the veteran fireman wept, he was calmly defiant. "Missing don't mean anything but missing," he said.

About 400 firefighters were missing and presumed dead, a numbing toll exacted on a tight fraternity. Entire ladder companies and squads were gone, including at

See FIREFIGHTERS, A22, Col. 1

Fear of Panic Prompts SEC To Ease Rules

U.S. stock markets are scheduled to reopen Monday, and federal regulators have agreed to bend the rules to let companies buy back their own shares if a flood of sell orders threatens a serious drop in prices.

BUSINESS, Page E1

■ Guide to coverage, A2

■ Latest updates, www.washingtonpost.com

After we returned to the compound, we immediately went back to the activities we were engaged in before the flag incident, but our morale was noticeably higher and our energy levels were renewed. Every interaction we had with the other organizations now was usually preceded by a comment like, "Hey, you guys are the ones who got that flag! Great job!" It was a timely morale boost to most of the workers.

Our work continued late into the evening on the night of the thirteenth. I made a final trip to the forensics lab at approximately 10:00 p.m. and the total count of recovered victims stood at approximately 112. That evening, as I drove back to Stafford, I thought about the flag, the additional sixty-four victims we recovered that day, and their family members and loved ones. I also thought about the resolve of the American people. Like the USMC flag recovered on the fourth floor, the American people are resilient and will survive. I prayed again for those who lost loved ones and for our nation's leaders.

I wanted to hold on to the positive images of the day. However, one picture I could not seem to get out of my head as I drove alone in my Jeep was that of a small pink tennis shoe, obviously from a young child. Earlier that day, I was asked to place the shoe inside one of the smallest child-sized body bags. As I mentioned earlier, by the evening of the thirteenth, we were able to recover some of the remains of the passengers of American Airlines Flight 77. Each time I viewed and handled these remains, I could feel energy and spiritual nutrients leaving my body. I could see the cold, distant, sorrowful look in the eyes of my co-workers—and in the mirror. While we experienced a momentary oasis from these feelings by recovering and delivering the USMC flag, each new body bag, especially the small ones designed for children, ripped at our emotions. Each time I unzipped these bags and verified the ID numbers, I could not help but think of my own children. On the ride home that evening and for the first time since watching my children come into this world, I felt my eyes well up with tears.

Alone in my Jeep, I spoke very frankly with God. I asked Him to reveal the good that could possibly come from such a tragedy. I was angry, sad, frustrated, and very, very tired. Couldn't He allow for at least one of those children to be spared? If the unscathed Marine Corps flag could inspire many of us, how much more would finding a survivor mean? I thought about a book I read a few years earlier. The book

When Bad Things Happen to Good People by Harold Kushner is dedicated to the memory of the author's fourteen-year-old son, who died from an incurable disease. Kushner, a religious leader of the Jewish faith, discusses why a good and loving God would allow so much pain and suffering in our world. The eventual conclusion is that suffering and the evil associated with it is not of God; however, God will use it to support His providential will. In some ways, there exists sadness so that we might appreciate joy; pain so that we will cherish pleasure; and untimely death so that we may see the gift of life in each new day. The next morning, I woke up with a better understanding and a sense of purpose. I vowed to treasure each day, grow closer to God, and live more purposefully. Months later, I found that Eric Jones and Chris Braman had undergone a very similar metamorphosis at about the same time.

By Friday, September 14, the morning traffic on I-95 was returning to normal. In fact, in order to get to the Pentagon within an hour, I needed to use the HOV (high-occupancy vehicle) lanes. I drove by the commuter lot, picked up a couple of my fellow "slugs," and drove to the Pentagon. Unlike Tuesday morning's ride, the vehicle was filled with lively conversation which centered around of the

9/11 tragedy. Additionally, one of the occupants had a copy of the *Washington Post*, and we discussed the story associated with the picture on the front page. For the next few days, Eric, Chris, Jared, and I were somewhat reluctant celebrities. I arrived at the compound at about 7:00 a.m. Friday morning, much later than the two previous days. That morning, the Department of Pentagon Security (DPS) had established an ID center that all workers were required to pass through. My pseudocelebrity status allowed me to move to the front of the line where I received my ID quickly and then linked up again with the morgue crew.

Also by Friday morning, the Army's Old Guard mortuary detail was now fully manned, in place, and preparing to phase out the Initial Response and Recovery Mortuary Team (IRRMT) I had helped to establish and support. That morning, members of the Old Guard and our crew worked side by side as LTC Edmonson and I introduced the Old Guard's leadership to the various points of contact they would need to interact with to carry out the recovery operations. By noon, we had brought out approximately twenty-two more bodies, bringing the total amount to about 134 victims recovered. It was obvious the army leadership was phasing in and wanted to assume the responsibilities of the remaining morgue duties. Eric, Chris, and I phased out our activities and by mid-afternoon, had transitioned to become advisors as opposed to doers. With more time on my hands, I decided to stop by the chaplain's tent and the trailers that housed the Red Cross and Salvation Army workers. I wanted to thank them for their outstanding support.

In the course of my conversation with one of the chaplains, he asked about the USMC flag and the duties we were performing with the morgue detail. The chaplain asked how I was dealing with the images of the bodies and handling their remains. I told him about the child's tennis shoe placed in the body bag the day before. I explained that the shoe reminded me of a pair my daughter owned, and could feel the emotions beginning to well up in me again. I shared with him the conversation I had with God on Thursday evening and the stronger sense of purposefulness and understanding I felt. Having completely transitioned my duties, I was essentially no longer needed at the compound and left the Pentagon at about 5:30 p.m. that afternoon to return home.

Chapter 4- The Aftermath

In the weeks and months following 9/11, Eric, Chris, and I remained in touch with each other. Eric was asked to join a group of firefighters from Northern Virginia who were going to New York to help relieve the exhausted FDNY (New York Fire Department) men and women. They had been working around the clock and needed the additional assistance. He spent the entire next week in New York at the World Trade Center site assisting and carrying out similar duties to the ones he performed at the Pentagon. The Army identified Chris Braman as one of the Pentagon heroes who assisted victims, such as Shelia Moody, immediately after the attack. The news of Chris's heroism, backed up by the media buzz created by the USMC flag photos, reached Congressman Curt Weldon's office. The Congressman was so moved by what he had read and heard of the story that he sought to have an entry placed into the congressional record to document the actions in and around the Pentagon on 9/11. Unfortunately, whoever did the research for him incorrectly included me as a participant in some of the rescue actions. Writing this book gives me an opportunity to set that portion of the record straight. I did not make it to the Pentagon in time to assist with rescue activities. My actions, as outlined in this book, centered on recovery operations, not rescue. I have reprinted the congressional record entry here:

The Congressional Record Entry

[Page: E1885] *GPO's PDF*

HON. CURT WELDON

OF PENNSYLVANIA

IN THE HOUSE OF REPRESENTATIVES

Friday, October 12, 2001

• Mr. WELDON of Pennsylvania. Mr. Speaker, I rise today to recognize the efforts of America's public safety and military personnel whose heroic actions at the Pentagon, the World Trade Center and the Pennsylvania site saved countless lives. As the Chairman of the House Armed Services Procurement Subcommittee and the founder of the Congressional Fire Services Caucus, I know well the overwhelming situations our civilian and military responders faced. That they persevered in the face of this tragedy is a testament to the dedication of these public servants.

• All of these personnel, whether local, state or federal, civilian or military, paid or volunteer, deserve the applause of this body. To highlight their combined efforts I wish to recognize three individuals. Their efforts represent the heroic actions of the thousands who responded to the calls for help on September 11 and throughout the days following the attack.

• Volunteer firefighter/paramedic Eric Jones, Army Staff Sgt. Christopher Braman, and Marine Corps Major Dan Pantaleo were featured rescuing a Marine Corps flag from the burning Pentagon on the front pages of newspapers and magazines around the world. It is this image that will remain in our memories as a symbol of American patriotism, unity and strength.

• In the days following the publication of their picture, they received many requests for press interviews. They declined each of these requests, because as true public servants, they neither expect nor desire any recognition for their efforts. What few know is that these individuals, through their countless acts of bravery, not only saved the flag, but also many Americans. At 9:40 A.M. on September 11 all three were called by destiny to perform heroic feats. As fire raged through the Pentagon, Mr. Jones, Staff Sgt. Braman, and Major Pantaleo rushed inside. These three men along with all the public safety and military personnel at the scene were responsible for rescuing hundreds of men and women injured by the explosion, the building collapse and burning jet fuel during the first minutes following the attack. After the injured had been saved, they remained on the site for many days to recover the bodies of those who perished.

I salute all Americans who answered the call for help on September 11. I am especially proud to highlight Eric, Christopher and Dan as examples of our public safety and military personnel whose contributions saved thousands from succumbing to the consequences of these terrorist attacks.

The Marine Corps flag we recovered from the fourth floor of the badly damaged Pentagon was given to officials at the National Aeronautics and Space Administration (NASA) and flown into space aboard the space shuttle *Endeavor* in May 2002. Also on that same flight was the huge American flag that was unveiled at the Pentagon during President Bush's visit; twenty-three shields (badges) of fallen NYPD officers; patches, posters, and an emblem from the FDNY; and patches from the Port Authority of New York and New Jersey. Additionally, six thousand small American flags to honor those lost and those who served in the response and recovery efforts for 9/11 were also flown aboard space shuttle *Endeavor*. Currently, the recovered USMC flag is encased and on display at the National Museum of the Marine Corps in Quantico, Virginia. It continues to serve as a reminder of our country's resilience.

Over the course of the next few days and months after 9/11, conspiracy theorists put forward the notion that the explosion and subsequent fire at the Pentagon was caused by a U.S. government missile. People, such as Steve Warren, have created web sites espousing this theory. As a firsthand witness to the conflagration at the site, I know for a fact it was an airplane. I saw parts of the plane that had sheared off just prior to, and during impact. I saw the remains of the victims that could have only come from a plane crash. Weeks later, DNA analysis confirmed the identities of the victims as those who boarded American Airlines flight 77. Providing any further attention to the agenda of those who seek to cause confusion or to divert blame from the al Qaeda sponsored terrorists would degrade the sacrifices of those who have bravely fought terrorism for the past ten years.

There are numerous examples of Americans who were inspired by 9/11 to fight terrorism. One example that strikes very close to home for me is my nephew, David Pantaleo. David celebrated his twenty-first birthday the day before the tragic attacks. He was in his second year of college and was seeking a pre-law degree, but after the attack on 9/11, he changed his major and ultimately graduated with a Master's degree in Homeland Defense. He began his service with the FBI in September 2007 and was working at the Bureau's Washington Field Office (WFO) at the time of his unexpected death. David, and thousands of other young men and women that chose to join in the fight against terrorism, are stellar examples of America's best.

In the months following 9/11, Chris Braman appeared on numerous television talk and magazine shows including *Oprah*. He was awarded the Soldier's Medal, the Army's award for life-saving, and a Purple Heart for the injuries he received from returning into the burning building. The Army leadership, through the recruiting command, thought Braman should tell his story to Americans, young and old alike, across the country. He went on a year-long tour of various speaking engagements. As Chris Braman has stated, "The story never changes." He went on to say, "They want to hear what happened because they were all affected that day. I tell everybody, I'm not a hero. In my eyes, I don't think I'm a hero."

Braman was diagnosed with post-traumatic stress disorder and has received help for it. Additionally, he was also diagnosed with a rare form of restrictive airway disease syndrome from the damage his lungs suffered during the rescue and recovery operations. It is a form of chemical pneumonia believed to have been caused by the hot toxins he inhaled. Like Eric Jones and I, Chris has reaffirmed his relationship with God in his search for inner peace and strength. He stated, "I look at life differently now. I was humbled that day and those three days I was there. When you look at death, it changes you. I was mentally, physically, emotionally humbled" (www.usma.edu/comm/PV/Pentagon.htm).

Due to Chris's notoriety, the 2002 Olympic Torch Relay Committee (OTRC) asked him to participate in the Olympic torch run in Washington, DC. On December 21, 2002, the Olympic torch was scheduled to be paraded across the Pentagon area and into the city of Rosslyn, Virginia. With a very large, cheering crowd lining the roads, Chris trotted with the torch along the area just outside the Pentagon compound. I, too, participated in the torch run and was proud to accept this honor. The flame was transferred to me about a quarter of a mile from the base of one of the most iconic statues in the DC area—the Iwo Jima memorial. It was a moving and humbling experience for me to run with the Olympic torch and to bring it to the base of that monument. For Marines, the Iwo Jima memorial stands as a symbol of unfailing perseverance, pride, and victory in the face of overwhelming odds.

In an equally inspiring ceremony, the OTRC asked Eric Jones to accept the torch the next day at a White House event that included President Bush and Liz Howell. Liz's husband, Brady Howell, was working as a management intern for the Department of Navy at the Pentagon and was killed on 9/11. The White House ceremony was an especially moving event. The President hugged Liz and gave a speech that struck the perfect balance of inspiration and hope, with care, concern, and sympathy for those lost in the 9/11 attacks. Symbolically, Eric wore two different shoes that day. On his left foot, he wore the same boot he wore the entire four days while working at the Pentagon. On his right foot was the shoe he wore while working at the WTC ground zero.

Olympic torch ceremony at the White House, December2001

A few days after the attack, an ad-hoc memorial was created near the base of the hill near the Navy annex. However, since then a design competition was held to determine the layout for the permanent monument to the 184 honored victims. Kaseman and Beckman, an architecture firm from Philadelphia, Pa., won the competition and the resulting memorial is both beautiful and heartrending. The memorial consists of 184 individual units designed in the form of benches, each dedicated to a victim. The units are located within the two acre area of the Pentagon that comprised the "ground zero" compound during the 9/11 timeframe. Each bench is engraved with a name of a victim and are arranged in accordance with the ages of the victims, starting with the youngest, Dana Falkenberg, a three-year old passenger on Flight 77. The engravings must be read either facing the Pentagon; memorializing those who were in the building at the time of the attack, or facing away from the building; for those who were aboard the plane. Each time I visit this site, I experience a deep sense of sadness.

The Pentagon Memorial

It has been said the attacks on September 11 were about symbolism. The terrorists wanted to attack symbols of American strength and power. They sought to change America and, symbolically, state to the rest of the world the United States was a weak nation. However, in the end they failed—miserably. The ensuing wars and regime changes in Afghanistan and Iraq have altered the political scene within the Muslim world for years to come. Over the past decade, American foreign policy has been one of engagement, inclusiveness, and cooperation with the Muslim community. The Muslim world is experiencing firsthand that America stands for freedom, democracy, and the sanctity of human rights. Recruitment for al Qaeda is suffering, and their previous worldwide support and influence has been diminished. The Taliban no longer occupies a place of legitimacy on the world stage. Their platform to recruit and influence the Muslim community is relegated to caves in remote regions of Afghanistan. Most recently, the youth-led uprisings in Egypt, Libya, and Tunisia demanding democratic elections and reforms have resulted in the toppling of the old regimes. The United States has never enjoyed a more favorable impression in Islamic countries, especially with younger Muslims and a policy of engagement is critical to maintaining this momentum.

Rest assured, however, the United States does bear scars from 9/11. Every time we see a TSA (Transportation Security Administration) agent at the airport, we are reminded of the 9/11 scars. Each time we visit the Pentagon and see the bench memorial to the victims lost that day, we are reminded of the 9/11 scars, and each time we visit New York and see the hole in the skyline which was once filled by two shimmering towers, we are reminded if the 9/11 scars. Over time, these scars will fade, but they should serve to offer us a reminder to be watchful and vigilant for the next asymmetrical attack.

A microcosm of our country's changes can be found in Chris Braman, Eric Jones, and me. Like our nation, in some form or another, we will also carry scars. For Chris, those scars manifest themselves in a form of PTSD. For Eric and me, they are less severe, but always there and just under the surface. A week after 9/11, on Tuesday, September 18, I participated in a luncheon at the JTRS JPO. As we were setting up the food for the luncheon, the event organizer asked me to retrieve a large five-gallon bucket of coleslaw from the refrigerator. As I opened the door to the refrigerator, the combination of the cool air and the smell of the coleslaw instantly took me back to working in the large white truck at the Pentagon compound. Even now, ten years later, I occasionally experience a smell or an image that takes my mind back to those four days I spent at the Pentagon. Perhaps most disturbing to me is the image of a small, dirty, child's tennis shoe, especially one with a pink stripe. So, while we each carry our own scars similar to the country as a whole, Chris, Eric, and I have moved on and live mindful of our commitments to balance our lives, continue in our spiritual journeys, and live with a sense of purposefulness. Eric Jones spent a week assisting in Haiti last year (2010) after that country's worst catastrophe in recorded history—the devastating 7.0 earthquake. I have become more active in my church and went on the adventure I had always talked about with my son; we ran with the bulls in Pamplona, Spain. Additionally, I spent time with both of my children at spiritual retreats. Chris Braman continues to maintain contact with Shelia Moody and occasionally makes speaking appearances to talk about being at the Pentagon on 9/11.

It is interesting to listen to people refer to first responders and those of us who worked side by side with them as "heroes" after 9/11. That is a label none of the people I worked with at the Pentagon would accept. The police officers and firefighters who rushed inside the towers in New York and into the burning Pentagon are extraordinary in every sense. In my mind, their actions are certainly commendable. Also laudable, were the actions carried out by every American who sought to contribute in some way—those who gave blood, volunteered to fight terrorism, or made a heartfelt monetary donation. For a moment in time, our country was united in purpose and cause. Millions of Americans played a role in solidifying our cohesiveness by placing the good of the country ahead of their individual everyday concerns.

Unfortunately, that unity is perishable. By the 2004 presidential election, national security was a secondary issue for most Americans and by the 2008 election it was a relegated to being a minor issue. I hope and pray our country never sees another day like September 11, 2001. However, if we do not allow the scars of that day to remind and unite us, we will become much more susceptible to similar, future attacks.

-----END----

Additional photos:

**Photo of 9-11 painting that hangs in the Reagan –
National airport in Washington DC
(USMC flag in the left side of the painting)**

Meeting the President at the Naval Academy, May 2001

Running with the bulls, Spain 2007

Acknowledgements

There are numerous people I want to thank for the encouragement, guidance, and mentorship that made this book possible. Starting with .... Lon Lawson, Mark Hevel, Col. Dan Choike, and Al McMichael -- your enthusiasm, positive outlook and encouragement were instrumental in assisting me to finish this book. A special thanks to those who read the book and offered input and recommendations; notably, Kerry Knowles, Mark Pizzo, Mark Thompson, Steve MacLaird, Tim Cassidy, Jeri-Lynn Smith, Mendy Sullivan, and Ms. Dozier. To the gang at CreateSpace –especially Lori the editor, well done, ma'am! To Dr. David Boyd- thank you, sir, for taking the time to meet with me.

A special thanks to an exceptional young lady, my graphic artist, Alexis Lowe – your patience and countless hours are very much appreciated!

To two exceptional men I had the pleasure to serve with during those four days – Eric Jones and Chris Braman – it was an honor to work with you.

To my family – starting with my parents, Al and Rose, thank you for your continuous love and support. To my brothers and sisters – much thanks for the never boring / dynamic

environment! To my daughter, Amanda and my son, Joe –
you make being a dad the best title I have ever held. To my
best friend and wife, Jackie: you bring out the best in me.
Always have.

Finally, to my Lord and Savior, Jesus Christ – I remain a
work in progress, but have learned that in Him all things are
possible.

About the Author

Dan Pantaleo retired from the Marine Corps in October, 2005 and currently serves as a Program Manager for BAE Systems, a Defense Contracting firm, and as an adjunct Professor at Strayer University. He received the Defense Meritorious Service Medal for his actions at the Pentagon. He is a member of the National Collegiate Athletic Association (Division III) Wrestling Hall of Fame and is an active member of his church, Stafford Crossing Community Church. Dan lists being a father to his two children, Joseph Michael and Amanda Marie, as his greatest accomplishment. He is married to the former Ms. Jacqueline Williams and they reside in Stafford, Virginia.

Email: danpantaleo@hotmail.com

Photo Credits:

1 – page 20,(personal collection), courtesy of DoD

2 – page 25, courtesy of Eric Jones

3 – page 27, courtesy of Chris Braman

4 – page 29 ,(personal collection)

5 – page 40, courtesy of DoD

6 – page 41, courtesy of DoD

7- page 42, courtesy of DoD

8 – page 44, Photo credits- Reuters/CORBIS

9 – page 52, courtesy of DoD

10 – page 54, (personal collection)/ courtesy of Eric Jones

11 – page 59, courtesy of Shipmate magazine

12 – page 62, courtesy of DoD

13 – page 64, Photo by George Bridges

14 – page 67, courtesy of Shipmate magazine

15 – page 69, courtesy of DoD

16 – page 72, Rights purchased from Getty Images

17 – page 87, courtesy of Eric Jones

18 – page 88, (personal collection)

19 – page 93 (personal collection)

20 – page 94 (personal collection)

21 – page 94 (personal collection)